walk away

silver heart

Poetry inspired by the Amy Lowell poem
'Madonna of the Evening Flowers'

A Love Poetry Trilogy
Book 1

Frank Prem

Publication Details

Published by Wild Arancini Press
Copyright © 2020 Frank Prem

All rights reserved:
No part of this publication may be reproduced, stored in a retrieval system, or transmitted in any form or by any means, electronic, mechanical, photocopying, recording or otherwise, without prior written permission from the publisher and author.

Title: *walk away silver heart*
ISBN: 978-1-925963-06-9 (pbk)
ISBN 978-1-925963-01-4 (e-bk)
February, 2020

For the poets who have gone before me.
May they ever continue
to inspire.

For my loved ones, all.

Contents

about a love poetry trilogy	1
Madonna of the Evening Flowers	2
walk away silver heart	3
a small piece (free)	5
well nourished (now to sleep)	7
from a confusion (of insensible things)	9
sough leaves and heartbeat moments (stolen)	11
been away (bearing home)	13
morning (awaited)	15
the way you wield (flashes in the light)	17
too much (to bear)	19
suddenly (the sun)	22
here	24
waiting	28
into day	30
I think (I paint)	32
finding me (a warm place carried)	34
murmuring (the lake)	36
need (goes on)	38
chiming a little tune (of you)	41
for the summer	43
bounds overrun (by aquilegias)	45
red and pink the blossom	46
tell me everything (about you)	48
walk away (silver heart)	50
and again	52
hide beneath (and burn)	54
lucky one	56
as though (always)	58
a muse for the madonna	61
one	63
two	64

three	65
four	67
five	69
six	71
seven	73
the original project	75
source materials	79
author information	81
other published works	83
what readers say	85
coming soon	91

about

a love poetry trilogy

Walk Away Silver Heart is the first of three poetry collections written for *A Love Poetry Trilogy*.

The origin of this work goes back a number of years to an occasion when I was fortunate to participate in a project that involved individual poets located around the globe.

Each poet chose a phrase from the body of a distinguished poem written long in the past, and used that phrase as inspiration for a piece of new poetry. New and old were then hyperlinked together to create an interactive work.

Over the course of the project three poems (and their poets) were chosen as source material for the experiment:

Amy Lowell – Madonna of the Evening Flowers (1919)
Walt Whitman – *Leaves of Grass* (1855) Parts 1 and 2
T.S. Eliot - *The Love Song of J Alfred Prufrock* (1915) (Epigraph plus Stanzas 1 – 5)

To the best of my knowledge no trace remains of the original project, but I was recently inspired to revisit and to continue an exploration of the effects these wonderful poems might have on my own work.

Each source poem commanded its own identifiable voice in my responses, and here I have worked with the Lowell poem.

In my reading, *Madonna of the Evening Flowers* was a love poem, written as a personal one-to-one communication from the heart. It had two distinct moods, reflecting initial absence of the beloved one, and then the Madonna in her element.

A lovely poem to read and contemplate.

Madonna of the Evening Flowers

All day long I have been working
Now I am tired.
I call: "Where are you?"
But there is only the oak tree rustling in the wind.
The house is very quiet,
The sun shines in on your books,
On your scissors and thimble just put down,
But you are not there.
Suddenly I am lonely:
Where are you?
I go about searching.

Then I see you,
Standing under a spire of pale blue larkspur,
With a basket of roses on your arm.
You are cool, like silver,
And you smile.
I think the Canterbury bells are playing little tunes,
You tell me that the peonies need spraying,
That the columbines have overrun all bounds,
That the pyrus japonica should be cut back and rounded.
You tell me these things.
But I look at you, heart of silver,
White heart-flame of polished silver,
Burning beneath the blue steeples of the larkspur,
And I long to kneel instantly at your feet,
While all about us peal the loud, sweet Te Deums of the Canterbury bells.

                                        Amy Lowell – 1919

walk away

silver heart

a small piece (free)

All day long I have been working

all the day
I
am working

toil
required to keep fuel
on the fire

and the table
well laden

I do
what I must
to ensure
all is
what it should be

yet
through each of those hours
I dream

inhabit
desire

and a yearning

to be home
to be with you

to be one
with my own spaces and places
well known

defined

all the day long
I have been
working as I know I must do
but
all the day long
too
I have nurtured
my heart

kept a piece
one small piece of it
free
and untrammelled
by need

or other
mundane requirement

I have placed it
in my mind
right there
beside you

our backs
warmed together
by fire

well nourished (now to sleep)

Now I am tired

I have gazed
up
at the sky
all morning

placed my nose
right in close
to smell
the sweet perfume
that comes
from blossom

in the garden
I have studied
the ways that green grass
grows

noting
that it did not move
at all
like this
in the winter

and listening
to birds
has taken more time
than anticipated

until
I find the day has fled
on wings
while I pursued it
on foot

I am tired now
with
nothing done

I am wearied
from my thoughts
and observations

I do believe
I need to rest
or
my senses may
explode

but this day

this wondrous day
has brought nourishment
for my soul

from a confusion (of insensible things)

I call: "Where are you?"

in the night

awakened
from a deep dream
that is a confusion
playing its dishevelment
as though a conversation
of insensible things
shared
between rational beings

my eyes open
staring at the darkness

startled

I call
where are you
but the silence is a hollow
swallowing sound and equilibrium
in a single gloating

I find that I am panting
and the feeling
of the heart
within my chest
is the gallop
of a panicked steed

I must rise
find the light switch

I need to feel the floor
unmoving
beneath my feet
as I stagger to the kitchen sink
to find a glass of water

to find a calming
that might last me through
until dawn

sough leaves and heartbeat moments (stolen)

But there is only the oak tree rustling in the wind

I
listen in the night
when you are gone
away

keep imagining
the car wheels
turning

the sound of gravel
crushed
beneath tyres

and I think that I can hear
the purring
of the engine

coming home

but no
you have hardly gone

the long hours
stretch
before me

and the sound
I can hear
is only the oak tree
rustling

as the wind
ruffles through
the sough leaves

I turn away

toss and roll

the bed
beneath me
has hardened

there is no comfort
to be had
from lying still
and wondering

about you
and the road

about the place
you are
and where you've been

the night to come
and the long hours
still
before me

the oak tree
sighs

the wind
is her accomplice

and every breath
she sounds
is another moment
taken

I will lose one more
the same
with every heartbeat
(at least)
until you get home

been away (bearing home)

The house is very quiet

been away

now
here I am

I cast my eyes
into the silence

nothing to see

the house
is very quiet

the hum
of a refrigerator
the only song

I walk
from room to room
to inspect the stillness

the hush

only
an arrangement
of teddy bears
is present

you have left them
to greet me

an interim
to hold

to tide me
over

I look around

the space is large

but the house
seems small

diminished
in spirit

every time
I journey
it is the same

only the soft fur
of the leading bear
can make
these first
empty moments
feel
like home

morning (awaited)

The sun shines in on your books

there is
a lazy ray
of sunshine

lying across the pages
of a philosophy

a
how to live
guide

pick it up
I
place it back down

it has become
a tedious thing

a randomness
of ideas
with you not here
to share it

and the stealthy sun
has crept away
its beam of light
dimmed
to dull
by increasing distance

the only philosophy
I can hold
right now
is getting through
each day

and wondering
what I should do
to fill the surplus minutes
every hour

until
with one last
gleam of fading sun

the night

becomes

and I
await
the morning

the way you wield (flashes in the light)

On your scissors and thimble just put down

I watch
the way you wield
your scissors

they flash in the light

attract my eye

and I see the threads
one by one
trimmed even

the needle darts
in its rhythmic
pattern

as the sewing machine
whirs

the replacement
of a button

a running repair
to my *outside* pants

become works
of an artisan craft
that I try to capture
together with your scissors
and your reels of cotton
on paper

with a pencil

but . . .

you are done
your tools
stowed

scissors in a box

needle
in its cushion

sewing machine
wheeled away
to a private corner

while I
run hands
through hair
contemplating a way
to stitch together
an opening line
to describe
this meditation

that catches my eye
as it flashes
in the light

needle
and cotton
and scissors

too much (to bear)

But you are not there

the chill
that touches
around my shoulders
is
a clue

the weight
within the silence
is another

I make a noise
while opening the door
but the quiet
dominates my sounds

I look around
momentarily
to find you

the hallway seems
a chasm
filled up
with emptiness
distilled

I look around
again
to find you

you're not there

you are
somewhere away

in sydney
this time

somewhere
beyond the great divide

when you said
you would be gone
for a few days
it didn't seem like
such an age

but you
are in sydney
and
this silence
is

too many minutes

too many hours

too many
days
and
just too much

you are coming
home
on the evening flight

the house
is waiting
and the soft plush bears
are waiting

the silence
is waiting

WALK AWAY SILVER HEART

and for this
soft bear
it is
just
too much

suddenly (the sun)

Suddenly I am lonely

suddenly
the cloud
appears

suddenly
the sun is gone

look around
I look around
at nothing

suddenly
the sound
is a bark

suddenly
dogs howling

listen
I listen hard
to sounds
akin to anger

and the day
has changed

the spark
is gone

what was sunshine
and gold
all at once
is grey

suddenly
I find

myself

suddenly
I am all
that is here

and suddenly in emptiness
I am lonely
and I wonder
what has changed

where
are you now

did you take my day
the sun
away
with you

suddenly

so
suddenly

here

Where are you?

I turn
to see you

you are not
there
anymore

I turn round
and
around again

seeking your shape
in the shadows

in footprints
across the floor

through the glass
slightly speckled
of the kitchen window
that leads my eye
outside

out
to the garden
where a shape
that is perhaps
just a shift of the sun
suggests
something of you

but
no
I don't think so

and I wonder
where have you gone

where are you
at this moment
when
I am seeking you
with a stray thought

an idea
that came into my mind

I
have a need
to share
to speak
to hear your reply
to this whim of mine

and I am
forlorn
for
I did not see you
depart

another sign
of my chronic
inattentiveness

I know

I know

I tell myself
berating

I must pay you
more mind

must notice where
you are going
what
you are doing
why it is
that you flit
from my mind
when I . . .

I preoccupy
the whole of me
with trivia

just trivia
that I believe might be
interesting

engaging to you

yet
I know
that is not so

it is not
really
so

and
all that is left
is to wait for you

quietly . . .

attentively . . .

thoughtfully . . .

distractedly . . .

absorbedly . . .

preoccupied-ly . . .

.
.
.

I am gone
inside myself
and my thoughts
again

you have returned
and I
did not notice
but suddenly you
are here

listening
to my story
which is now gushing out
not at all rational

you are here
and you listen

and
I think
that you know
everything
that there is
to know

about me

waiting

I go about searching.

the day begins

alone

I wander
around the house

perform
perfunctory tasks

clean away
the dishes

rake the grate
and set
the fire

but
do not light it

this becomes a search
for
new purposes

.
.
.

today

today

it has only been
an hour
or two

it will only be
a day

but
so long
is a moment
stretched in time

so very long
is the passage
of a cloud that moves
relentlessly
across the sky

from west
to east

I would turn
the day back
to not so long ago

east
to west
or push it
forward
to the next time

I search
myself
this time
for meaning

and
finding none
wander empty

through room
after room

into day

Then I see you

and today
the clouds
come low

grey
surrounds my head
covers
my eyes

I walk
in blindness

stumbling forward

touch
replaces sight

what I feel
is all I see

and all I touch
is cloud
is grey
to my senses

I
walking blind

in the heart
of nothing

then
you
are revealed

sun
is stronger
than cloud

it is you
in the light

the night
becomes day
and . . .

I see you

I think (I paint)

With a basket of roses on your arm

I think
of summer

leaves open
like
a fluttering of flags
to adorn
deciduous trees

I think
a pastel t-shirt

and think the wide brim
of a straw sunhat
too

barefoot
lightly upon a path

a twirl
with a basket full
of picked greens
and vegetables

I watch my thought
skip
and dance

watch
those leaves

I paint the straw hat
establish
the t-shirt

dab the zucchini

you

paint your green leaves
too

finding me (a warm place carried)

Standing under a spire of pale blue larkspur

I
beneath the pandorea

even
standing at my tallest
it towers above me

a floral wall
of hanging bells
in
creamy white

you are one
with the secateurs
cutting where you will

your ornaments

adornments
and pretties
for arrangement

a vase

you seem
to stop
your arm stilled
eyes fixed
on me

I am something . . .
something . . .
not expected

I wait on you

your leisure

the time needed
for a surprise
to pass
and you to raise me

like a talisman
a love mote
from the garden

a warm place
to be carried
close
to where *you* are

where you *live*

the being
of you

made more

more
than one pandorea
of cream
and white

murmuring (the lake)

You are cool, like silver

the water stills
as though
it has never
been disturbed

strange

I watch the place
where you submerged

see reflections

it is evening
and the moon
is rising hugely
on the horizon

the water shimmers
a trail of light
murmuring
even in the stillness

and you arise
cool to touch
right before my eyes

a personification
of the silver night

and laughing
while the water
streams

in rivulets
of moonshine

behind you
the water shimmers
to its own
murmurings

need (goes on)

And you smile

I become
a thing
of need

a hunger in the night time
ravening

desiring

and wanting

a rampage
when I'm standing still

emotions
all the time
racing

running

leaping
while I fear
I'll fall

fear
that I have fallen
already

deep
delves each feeling
each pounding
pummelling
of uncontrolled
sensation

and I don't know
what I
should do

don't know
how
to create calm space
that I might fall
in
to

and you smile
at me

have me wondering
did I see
what I saw

did it mean
what I thought

was it intended
for me

do you smile
like that
at everyone

at anyone

at someone else . . .

I become a thing
that is fully lost

I become a doubt

no trust
or faith
just gnawing

and still
I need . . .

something

still I want . . .

something

still
I long

still I hope

still
I wish . . .

for something

and go on
bleeding

chiming a little tune (of you)

I think the Canterbury bells are playing little tunes

I think
that I heard the bells
as you
brushed past

playing little
tinkling
riffs

when they touched

one
into
the next one
rang

and one
again

into another

ting
tong
tang

as I listened
I believe I heard
a small tune
of you

yes

I believe
I heard them sing
your name

ting

ting-a-ling

tang
tong
tang

and *ting*

ting

tang-a-lang tong

they sang your name

at least
that
is what I heard

the breeze
when I closed my eyes
was like
your fingers
wandering
through my hair

and as it ruffled me
I heard the bells . . .

ting tang
tang
tong

. . . call aloud
your name

for the summer

You tell me that the peonies need spraying

and now
with the spring season
upon us
and the summer
set
to bloom hot and dry
and long
you point me
towards the new garden bed

especially
the pineapple sage
that bloomed
so prolifically
in its first year

its need for care

if the whole of the bed
is to grow
as we have planned
room must be made

for the pittosporum
to hedge
and the waratahs
to transform
from seedling
to tree

through every season
we must tend
these things
that we so
love

snipping

touching

and inhaling

there is joy
in this

joy that comes
from your hand
and mine
tilling with our fingers

moulding
with implements

at the approach
of summer

bounds overrun (by aquilegias)

That the columbines have overrun all bounds

the aquilegias
have restless hearts

they have burst
beyond their bounds

we should have known
they would be
beyond containing

pretty flowers
they respond
to love

and water
and fertilizer

are they not
like you
and me

and
do we not
bloom
beneath the warming sun

a fair
display

of
you and I

red and pink the blossom

That the pyrus japonica should be cut back and rounded

I broke
a branch
off the japonica

I have always thought
the red
quite beautiful

I find
specimens
in odd corners
of strange gardens
that I pass by
on the street

not cut back
or rounded
but growing wild

a little
unkempt

I grasp a branch
work it
to and fro
to break free

the red blossoms
in my hand
are a picture

and
in another place
another
ignored backyard tangle
there is a neglected peach

a prettiness
of petals
and stamens

I bring them home
and hope
that you will know
what I was thinking

when I chose
each branch of blossom
for you

tell me everything (about you)

You tell me these things

talk to me

tell me things
you think
I need
to know

pour your ideas
red
into my wine glass

speak of love

talk in tongues
of fire

tell me of your anger

of the passion
that is the same thing

shout aloud
all the things
that *you* believe
hold meaning

I will turn them
with a flourish
of phrasing
into a word song

ta-da ta-da-da

throw your glass
into the fire

then
start dancing

tell me
all these things

I
would know
everything
and all there is

about you

walk away (silver heart)

But I look at you, heart of silver

silver heart
I look at you

see myself
as
I should have been

but something pure
was lost
along the way

I don't glance
backward
do not check my stride
but

I look at you
heart of silver
and wonder why you
look at *me*

I believe
you see my
might have
and my *could*

if some small part
of you
were surrendered
to become a part
of me

you choose
not to see
what I have been
and done

WALK AWAY SILVER HEART

but only catch
the darkness
in my eyes

and fall
into a dream
of me

silver heart
I look at you . . .
and wonder

will you walk
away

and again

White heart-flame of polished silver

I hear
the song

I have heard it now
almost
forever

your lustred hair
has changed a shade
or two
from
copper shine
to this smooth
and polished
silver

but not the song

your voice
is young
still
and again

I hear it
as a young man hears

for that
is how it comes
to me

a white purity
of sound
that goes straight
to my heart

right to
where I feel
these things

and I know
that
even though I
am age clumsy

and age foolish

even though I am
age blind
to what surrounds me
in these hasting times

when I hear you
sing
that song that we both
know

I am
a youth

only a youth
again

hide beneath (and burn)

Burning beneath the blue steeples of the larkspur

I
burn lightly
brightly

underneath
the helianthus
I burn
and I hide

and then
the yellow-gold
crinkles into brown

my smoke
becomes
the sky

and the grey descends
to cover me over
as I

burn
beneath

I aspire
and I
desire

open up
my heart
right on my sleeve

where you can
easily
see what I wish

what I
believe

beneath a helianthus
spike
I
I
I

burn higher

I burn again higher

and higher

underneath
the sun

is where I
hide

lucky one

And I long to kneel instantly at your feet

wake
to a shining day

no smoke
no cloud
to play before
my eyes

look across the sky
to the gold
and to the blue

look
all around

earth green and brown

and then I see
a shape I know

busy in the garden

busy
with the singing

busy with
the life that comes
of breathing air
like this

radiating
all
that is good

and I want to throw
myself
down onto my knees
right there
at your feet

these are those days
such
shining days

days
when I know
without a doubt
that
the lucky one
is me

as though (always)

> *While all about us peal the loud, sweet Te Deums of the Canterbury bells*

when the bellringers
for the granite-built cathedral
up on the town's hill
begin their practice

it will be a tuesday evening

always
it is on a tuesday
in the evening

and
I won't notice them
at first

not at all

but they
will know me

yes
they will know me
subconsciously

like a song
seated
back of mind
influencing
without
acknowledgement

so it is
that the music of the bells
is in me
and I do not know
but
begin to respond

my movements
become
differently fluid

thoughts divert
from where they were
to assume
a kind
of rhythm

reflective
of the clapper sounds
that I cannot yet hear

so that
when my ears
at last
have become attuned
there is no
new knowledge
involved

for I have been
all the while
aware

all the while
un-aware
and yet affected

until my whole being
is encompassed
in the sweet loud sound
of te deums
ringing out
and all around me

and it is
as though
this
has always been

a muse

for the madonna

one

sun rises
falls
across your books

physiology
texts
with illustrations

muscle and grist

fascia
and radiating red
depict
the secrets
of a body

I have not
slept well

pace the hallway
the kitchen

subconsciously listening
for a sound of you

who are away
at your studies

walking other paths

beneath
a different sun

two

the breeze
roaming idly
through the oak tree leaves
brings to mind another sound
from a lifetime ago

a voice
never heard before

with an insistent demand
for my attention
to a song
and a singer

the suggestion of a place
to be

an idea
of a someone

me . . .

and a someone . . .

perhaps . . .

me
instantly bereft

in the sure certainty
of non-attraction

lost
before begun

three

the glancing sun
notes the thread
and cloth
of a tapestry

quarter made

abandoned

quarter made
again

a small thing
I do

I know you like it

admire each
of my miniscule progressions
in a persistence
that has carried me
for years

the stitches transform
to your delight
into an image

there comes a point
when I too can see
what it is
that is emerging

but
my pleasure
lies in the way
that you respond

I stitch
for your joy

for now
though
you are gone
while the cloth
lies strewn
on the sewing table

and the house
is completely quiet

filled with the hum
of the refrigerator

the birds outside

the traffic
rolling by

there is hardly room
for loneliness
in this intense silence

but
I have become aware
again
of what it is
to be by myself

four

I grind the coffee

you are there
rising up
before me

in the aroma
of this ritual that we live
lies a way
in which
we come alive
within the singing steam
of a percolation
on the stove top

and
in the steam
today
I am seeing you
at work

clay
in your hands

modelling a talisman
a minor imp

a devil

a fallen angel

bake him brown
then
paint him
black

and set him
demon guardian
to watch
the doors

five

place your fingers
on the fretboard

place your fingers
to pluck
the strings

let your voice carry
to the garden

I will tend
seedlings
to your song

they grow and flower

seed

self sow

spread
to fill
all the empty spaces

perhaps they move
to the seasons
of your silver tune

I will cut them back
leave
a little room
for other things

you will tell me
what you most desire
to grow

will tell me all
that you wish

six

the next book should be
an anatomy
of the heart

not the muscle

but the emotional
existence
that is
we

and is
us

the next
should be a book
of flame

heat
that will not burn
but
can bring me
to my knees
at your feet

to rest my head
upon you

and
to hold your hand
even now
each time we go out

wherever
we walk

life
is a song
you know

I hear you
singing

life is a song

I know

I know

and this
is the song
of me

seven

and I see you
as though from above

where you go
I must follow

if not by footstep
then
by desire

by wish

by thought and picture
held tight
to me

as though
my sole
remaining passion

and
so it is

for what is there
if there is not
this

what am I
if I am not
of you

this love
is a silvery song

a harmony

I hold the note

I keep the place

I mark the time

sing again

the original project

My initial responses and submissions (written for the project in around 2001) were the poems *cool, like silver* and *the sun shines in on your books,* which I have included below. It will be easy, I think, for a reader to identify them as work from an earlier phase of my writing career.

the sun shines in on your books

The sun shines in on your books

I immerse myself in your pictures,
sketched in the clarity of cold
night without moon. Sharpness of
line and image.
You draw me in, watching
the pale detail of a white lily emerge
beneath your hand. Erupted
yellow, the core.

I am walking in your world,
a journeyman of word reflections
from the mirror pools of observation
and chance encounter,
marked by typeface on white paper.
Mood and manner, mind and heart.
Extracts from the seizure of a moment
frozen in time.

I watch you move around your drawings,
from the near side of the bed,
as the sun streams in on your books,
on your folio,
and on your body bent to raise
the lily in the slow light of morning.
I picture you in words.

cool like silver

You are cool, like silver

Cool, she was, like silver. Dapples
on the rolling, falling waters
of a stream come out of sunrise,
sliding to glisten. On the rocks
as smooth as thigh out-stretched,
she taught the way. To reach
and to become as one
with flowing water, to know its secrets
and the treasure of eddied places,
to slow measure a path across the bed,
through rapids and turbulence. Don't
rush, don't fall.

Cool she was, like silver trapped
or caught. Inside a playground of
the moon, under a soft light and
shining. A waving dance
of shimmers, to mesmerise. Me?
I was lost. In time, control,
and knowledge far too early. For
the coolness of her silver
purchased only one long shiver. I
could not heed, nor halt. So fast,
too fast expired, I could not slow and
I, could not go on.

source materials

If you would like to find some information about the life of Amy Lowell and her writing, a good place to start is her entry in Wikipedia:
https://en.wikipedia.org/wiki/Amy_Lowell

I have accessed the source poems for this project from the following online locations:

The Reader (Lowell):
https://www.thereader.org.uk/featured-poem-madonna-of-the-evening-flowers-by-amy-lowell/

The Walt Whitman Archive (Whitman):
https://whitmanarchive.org/published/LG/

The Poetry Foundation (T. S. Eliot):
https://www.poetryfoundation.org/poetrymagazine/poems/44212/the-love-song-of-j-alfred-prufrock

I commend these organisations, and the work of the selected poets to you.

FP
2020

author information

About Frank Prem

Frank Prem has been a storytelling poet since his teenage years. He has been a psychiatric nurse through all of his professional career, which now exceeds forty years.

He has been published in magazines, online zines and anthologies in Australia, and in a number of other countries, and has both performed and recorded his work as spoken word.

He lives with his wife in the beautiful township of Beechworth in North East Victoria, Australia.

Did you enjoy this book?

If you have enjoyed reading *Walk Away Silver Heart*, please take a moment to do two small things.

First, leave a short review of this book on Amazon by visiting **https://mybook.to/Walk_Away_Silver_Heart** and clicking on the button (near the bottom of the page) that is labelled "Write a customer review."

Online reviews provide social proof to readers and are critical to support Indie authors.

The second thing is, please visit Frank Prem's Webpage at **https://FrankPrem.com** and sign up to join his Newsletter list. From time to time the Newsletter will let you know what is happening with Frank and his writing, as well as keeping you informed of any giveaways that might be planned.

Linkages to other writing and storytelling activities (such as YouTube videos) can be accessed from the Webpage.

other published works

Frank Prem

Small Town Kid (2018)
ISBN: 978-0-9751442-3-7 (pbk)
ISBN: 978-0-9751442-4-4 (e-bk)

Devil In The Wind (2019)
ISBN: 978-0-9751442-6-8 (pbk)
ISBN: 978-0-9751442-7-5 (e-bk)

The New Asylum (2019)
ISBN: 978-0-9751442-8-2 (pbk)
ISBN: 978-0-9751442-5-1

With Other Authors

Herja, Devastation - With Cage Dunn (2019)
ISBN: 978-1-925905-04-5 (pbk)
ISBN: 978-1-925905-03-8 (e-bk)

Short Stories of Forest and Fantasy: Fantasy Anthology by OzTales(2019)
ISBN: 978-0-9872863-7-6 (pbk)
ISBN: 978-0-9872863-5-2 (e-bk)

Aquarius: Speculative Fiction Inspired by the Zodiac (The Zodiac Series) by Deadset Press
ISBN: 978-1393586371 (pbk)

what readers say

Small Town Kid

A modern-day minstrel

As a 'New Australian' of eastern European heritage, much of Frenki's life resonates with me, and yet it's the imagery of time and place that makes these poems familiar to all Australians. And perhaps to non-Australians as well. Boyhood and the wonder years. Some things are universal. Highly recommended

—A. F. (Australia)

Small-Town Kid is a wonderful collection
With so few words Frank is able to paint a picture so vivid you can't help but get lost in the story. Whether he's talking about family, a picnic, a trip to the butcher or even the outside toilet it's difficult not become immersed in the words and imagine yourself right there with him. Cover to cover, this is an excellent read.

—S. T. (Australia)

A poet's walk through his childhood in a small Australian town. From the dedication poem, 'I Can Hardly Wait to Show You', to 'Circular Square Town', Frank Prem's chronological journey from infancy to the present has a familiar feel to it, almost as if you were taking a walk through your own memory lane to recall the innumerable small, but unforgettable moments that make up a life.

—J. L. (USA)

Devil In The Wind

I live in the US, and though I recall these fires, I never knew the personal stories behind them. Frank Prem instantly grips you by the throat in his step-by-step story of survival.
I was especially taken because he told the story through poetry, which I've never related to this way. It was stark and vivid, the language of a survivor. It's a quick read, but trust me, this book will stay with you.

Bravo!

—K. K. (USA)

Very moving, beautiful, and terrible

—J. S. (South Africa)

Outstanding!
I'm not normally a reader of poetry, but Devil in the Wind captured the essence of 7 February 2009, and the days and weeks afterwards, with eloquence and ease. Beautifully written, the author has given a human voice to those who matter. Highly recommended.

—B. T. (Australia)

The New Asylum

Brilliant succinct memoir. These insightful, thought provoking behind-the-scene stories are woven so seamlessly you'll lose track of time. 'this somebody's boy' is one of many which will hold your heart.

__M.P-B. (Australia)

Words can't do justice to the emotional journey I travelled in (reading this collection). I don't think anything can. My heart bled, my eyes burned. And I will read it again, to remind me.

__C. D. (Australia)

"The eternal asylums of mental health ...another shift in the backwards."
If I had to pick one book over the past year that has truly resonated with me, this would be it. It's a hauntingly beautiful window into the successes and failures of working with the mentally disabled, and the impact on the human psyche. ( )

__K. B. (USA)

Herja, Devastation

How does a reader give this work the credit it deserves? Simply written, powerfully felt. A man with a job, a woman he loves beyond sanity (or is it his only hold on sanity?).
He is her tool, he says, and I feel the depth of that longing to be nothing more than that. Loved it. Can't say that enough.

__C. (Australia)

The cover alone was enough to excite me to look inside. I'm glad I did.
I loved this book. I don't know whether to call it poetry or prose, and I'd never heard of Eddic tales, but if that's your thing, or you want to feel the subtle menace, albeit from a loving hand.
This is a book I will reread and remember for a long, long time.

__C. (Australia)

As a combination of poetry, prose, and wonderfully ominous illustrations, I found Herja, Devastation refreshingly original. The narrative slipped seamlessly between the two forms and the valkyrie/assassin story carried my interest throughout. Highly recommended!

—G. B. (Australia)

coming soon

A Kiss For The Worthy

Part 2 of **A Love Poetry Trilogy** is *a kiss for the worthy* and features love poems inspired by Walt Whitman's *Song of myself (Leaves of Grass)*.

Rescue and Redemption

Part 3 of **A Love Poetry Trilogy** is *rescue and redemption*, and features love poems inspired by T.S. Eliot's *The Love Song of J. Alfred Prufrock*.

FrankPrem.com

www.ingramcontent.com/pod-product-compliance
Lightning Source LLC
Chambersburg PA
CBHW071747080526
44588CB00013B/2173